Transatlantic Slavery: An Introduction

INTERNATIONAL
SLAVERY
MUSEUM

National Museums Liverpool

LIVERPOOL
UNIVERSITY PRESS

Contents

Reverend Jesse Jackson with Dr David Fleming and
Dr Richard Benjamin at the International Slavery Museum.
© Simon Webb

Foreword by Reverend Jesse Jackson

From the time that three Englishmen, John Lok (1555), William Towerson (1556) and especially Sir John Hawkins (1562), initiated British involvement in the slave trade, until it was ended by Parliament in 1807, Liverpool stood as an important if grotesque transit point.

It is estimated that 40% of the world's slave trade passed through the city's docks. While Liverpool was also a centre of other British commercial shipping interests, the slave trade thus played a vital role in the city's development as a thriving metropolis.

The eternal shame of world history is that Africans were the 'commodities' being shipped and traded under inhuman and immoral conditions.

Modern Britain would not have been possible without the industrial revolution and slave labour. The enslavement of Africans fuelled the economic development of the US and the world – so in that sense, African people, whether in the US or in Britain, are creditors, not debtors. From finance to cotton, shipping and trade, no economic development in the world could have evolved without the contributions – as enslaved people – of African people. Quotes at the Museum ring like a freedom bell to me:

'Remember not that we were bought, but that we were brave... not that we were sold, but that we were strong.'

When I travelled to London, Bristol, Liverpool and nine other cities with Equanomics UK in 2007 – in part to commemorate the 200th anniversary of the abolition of the Slave Trade Act in the UK – I could not help but witness the contemporary legacy of slavery that permeates all facets of British life today. The structural inequalities faced by today's descendants of Africa in education, criminal justice, jobs and employment, access to capital and credit remind us every day of the legacy of slavery in today's world. And so it is no wonder that Liverpool is also noted for its tradition of slave rebellions and resistance to racism – from the 1919 rebellion to the protests against unemployment and police discrimination in the 1980s.

The Beatles' rhythm and blues 'sound' grew out of Memphis and Mississippi as much as it did from Liverpool – regions on both sides of the Atlantic sharing great kinship in their musical traditions. Memphis and Mississippi were the home of the blues for legends Muddy Waters, B. B. King, Bobby Bland and Elvis. And no doubt the Beatles' music, lyrics, themes and even song titles drew inspiration from the centuries-long roots and cultural influences of Liverpool's African people.

And who would know, without the excellent research of the International Slavery Museum, that Penny Lane, popularised by the Beatles, was named after a famous slave trader?

The Museum documents the economic and inhumane exploitation of Africans, collects and houses the artefacts of slavery and also provides progressive educational programmes about the critical legacy of slavery in

This list describes the sale of 268 slaves imported into Jamaica on the Liverpool ship *African* in September 1794. The sale of the Africans raised over £9,000.

The Black Achievers Wall in the International Slavery Museum is a celebration of Black Achievers past and present.
Photograph: Lee Garland.
© National Museums Liverpool/ Redman Design

human, moral and financial terms. It highlights aspects of British complicity with other countries in the trade and also prominent abolitionists who were important in its demise.

In this sense, the Museum stands as a global memorial to those enslaved Africans who not only suffered the depths of human debasement through this trade but who, in the process, contributed greatly to the development of Western civilisation.

As a visitor to and Patron of the Museum, as well as someone who greatly appreciates its work, I am pleased to encourage all to visit this important institution. The impact of slavery is not to be relinquished to 'the history of the past', but is a part of the continuous struggle of today, the 'right here and now', to forever eradicate the inequities carried over from the historical enslavement of African people.

The International Slavery Museum in Liverpool brings this message to life, and is truly a treasure to the global community.

Rev. Jesse L. Jackson, Sr.
President and Founder
Rainbow PUSH Coalition

What is slavery?

These mutilated children were victims of atrocities committed in the Congo Free State (now Democratic Republic of Congo) in around 1905. Yoka's (standing) right hand was amputated, whilst Mola lost both hands to gangrene after they were bound too tightly by mercenaries. © Anti-Slavery International

Slavery is a form of forced labour in which people become the property of others. Slaves are held against their will from the time of their capture, purchase or birth, in a destructive relationship in which other people have absolute power over them. Slaves are deprived of the right to leave, to refuse to work, to own property or to receive reward or compensation, such as wages.

Evidence of slavery pre-dates written records, and has existed to varying degrees in almost all ages, cultures and continents. In some societies, slavery existed as a legal institution or socio-economic system, but today it is formally outlawed in nearly all countries around the world. Nonetheless, slavery continues in various forms and millions still suffer.

Freedom from slavery is an internationally recognised human right. Article 4 of the Universal Declaration of Human Rights states that

'No one shall be held in slavery or servitude; slavery and the slave trade shall be prohibited in all their forms.'

The International Labour Organization estimates that *at least* 12 million people are in forced labour around the world. These people have no rights, are treated as objects, and are at the mercy of their 'employers'. Where forced labour is used, other human rights abuses frequently take place, including rape, torture and murder.

This tin glazed earthenware tile is transfer printed in black. It depicts a Turkish merchant instructing a Black slave.

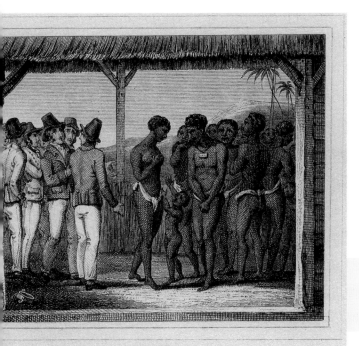

Slaves exposed for Sale.
See Bickells' West Indies as they are, page 19 &c.

European buyers haggle over a group of enslaved Africans, 'exposed for sale' at a slave auction.
© Anti-Slavery International

Anti-Slavery International reports that the main types of modern slavery are:

BONDED LABOUR: people are forced or tricked into taking out a loan and are forced to work very long hours to repay the debt. They receive basic food and shelter but may never pay off the loan, which can be passed down for generations.

EARLY AND FORCED MARRIAGES: women and girls are married without choice or consent and forced into lives of servitude, often with physical violence.

FORCED LABOUR: people are illegally recruited by individuals, governments or political parties, usually under threat of violence or other penalties.

SLAVERY BY DESCENT: people are either born into a slave class or are from a 'group' that a society views as suited to being used as slave labour.

TRAFFICKING: the transport and/or trade of people from one area to another for the purpose of forcing them into conditions of slavery.

WORST FORMS OF CHILD LABOUR: according to the International Labour Organization, an estimated 126 million children around the world work in conditions harmful to their health and welfare, with 8.4 million in conditions of slavery.

Untitled #31, Missing Series, 2007/8 is one of a series of photographs by Rachel Wilberforce. The images depict scenes of sex-trafficking and prostitution; a slave trade which still thrives today.
© Rachel Wilberforce

Young boys working at a brickworks in the Punjab, India.
© Anti-Slavery International

A history of transatlantic slavery

> 'Africa will write its own history, and it will be, to the north and to the south of the Sahara, a history of glory and dignity.'
>
> PATRICE LUMUMBA, FIRST PRIME MINISTER OF THE CONGO, 1961

The story of transatlantic slavery is a fundamental and tragic human story that must be told, retold, and never forgotten. Africa and its peoples are central to this story.

People in many parts of Africa still perform masked dances on important ceremonial occasions. This example is a gelede or dance mask from the Yoruba people of Nigeria. The mask is always worn with a costume that both hides and transforms the wearer's identity.

African pasts

Africa is a vast continent, home to hundreds of millions of people and full of rich and diverse cultures. Africa is also the cradle of civilisation, and archaeological evidence has shown that we are all descendants of Africans.

West Africa, from where Europeans seized most victims for the transatlantic slave trade, covers an enormous area. It stretches all along the Atlantic coast of the continent and inland for hundreds of miles. Within this huge area are many diverse cultural groups, each shaped by its environment. The Fulani, Hausa, Igbo, Akan and many other peoples developed sophisticated cultures long before the arrival of Europeans in the fifteenth century.

The Africa 'discovered' by Europeans in the fifteenth century was neither backward nor barbarous compared with Europe. It was simply different.

Through cultural, political, social and religious systems as well as inventions in agriculture, ceramics and metalworking, Africans shared in some of the great cultural transformations of world history.

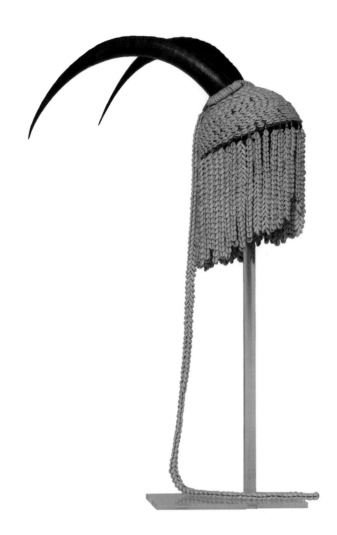

This late 19th century figure is from Portuguese Congo (now called Cabinda, an enclave of Angola). It shows a high-status woman, possibly the mother of a chief. Africans still sculpt wooden figures for many different reasons. They were commonly made to commemorate important ancestors or for shrines devoted to spirits.

ABOVE: Cowrie shells, like those used in this headdress, came originally from the Maldive Islands in the Indian Ocean. They were used as currency in many areas of West Africa. Former slave Olaudah Equiano tells of being sold for 172 cowrie shells.

This is a skin-covered cap mask from Ejagham, South East Nigeria and dates from the late nineteenth century. Cap masks like this were worn by dancers at the funerals of important elders. This mask has both a black and a white face.

The trade triangle was a route linking Europe, Africa and America. European capital, African labour and American land and resources combined to supply a European market with the raw materials it demanded.

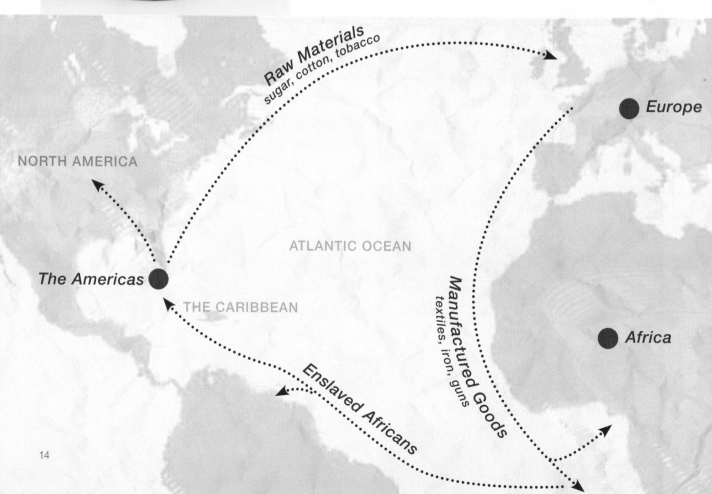

Raw Materials
sugar, cotton, tobacco

● **Europe**

NORTH AMERICA

ATLANTIC OCEAN

The Americas ●

THE CARIBBEAN

Manufactured Goods
textiles, iron, guns

● *Africa*

Enslaved Africans

The International Slavery Museum features a recreation of a
traditional Igbo family compound.

Photograph: Lee Garland. © National Museums Liverpool/Redman Design

African Hospitality by J. Morland (1761) illustrates a verse in which Africans have bravely rescued Britons from a storm at sea. The writer of the poem wonders if the Britons will show similar mercy to the Africans.

Slave Trade by the same artist (1761) illustrates a verse in which an African family is split and sold to diffferent slave traders.

'Europe undertook the leadership of the world with ardour, cynicism and violence.'

FRANTZ FANON, PSYCHIATRIST AND POLITICAL WRITER, 1961

Why Africans?

Europeans began exploring West Africa during the fifteenth century, even before they discovered the Americas. Almost immediately, Portuguese traders began to enslave Africans, and it was not long before Africans were being forcibly transported across the Atlantic Ocean to work in the American colonies of the European nations.

Europeans considered the achievements of their own civilisation to be paramount, and used their own rigid ideas of civilisation to justify the enslavement and abuse of Africans.

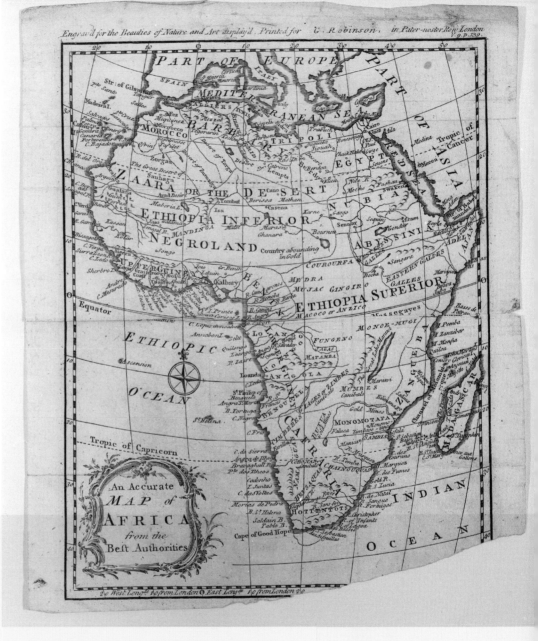

'An accurate map of Africa from the best authorities', drawn in London in the eighteenth century. The ports and rivers of West Africa are especially detailed.

The TOBACCO-MANUFACTORY in different Branches.

Tobacco was a labour-intensive crop grown mainly in North America. 'The Tobacco Manufactory in different Branches' (1750) shows how it was harvested.

CUTTING THE SUGAR-CANE

'I am apt to suspect the Negroes to be naturally inferior to the Whites. There scarcely ever was a civilised nation of that complexion, nor even any individual, eminent either in action or in speculation. No ingenious manufactures among them, no arts, no sciences.'

DAVID HUME, PHILOSOPHER AND SCIENTIST, IN HIS ESSAY 'OF NATIONAL CHARACTERS', 1753

Because African societies and culture were unfamiliar, Europeans simply denounced the whole continent. They considered it to be a barbaric place, overrun with savage tribes and religious despotism. These racist beliefs would later be used as a justification for colonial involvement in Africa.

This painting by William Jackson (active about 1770-1803) is of the *Watt*, built by Edward Grayson of Liverpool in 1797 for the local merchant firm of Watt and Walker. She was equipped with 22 guns and was built for the Jamaica trade, where Richard Watt also had an estate. She continued in the West Indies trade, principally carrying sugar, until 1812.

Why slavery?

When European explorers 'discovered' the Americas in the fifteenth and sixteenth centuries, they quickly exploited the new lands and their peoples for the resources they found there.

The Portuguese began growing sugar in Brazil in the 1540s. As demand for sugar grew in Europe, plantations were established in the European colonies in the Caribbean. Other profitable commodities were also grown in the plantation system, including cotton, coffee and tobacco, and demand for these grew as well.

Sugar-growing required a large workforce. It was hard, heavy work. Local labour was scarce because millions of indigenous peoples had died after the colonisation of their lands by Europeans. Many were killed in battle, trying to repel the invaders. Others were worked to death, especially in the mines. European diseases such as influenza and smallpox wiped out huge numbers more.

So European colonists looked to the continent of Africa for a new supply of labour. Initially, Portugal and Spain took the lead in developing the transatlantic slave trade, to be followed later by England, France and the Netherlands.

This resulted in the largest forced migration in human history. Africans were enslaved in their millions and transported across the Atlantic Ocean to the Americas to work on European plantations.

Manillas are horseshoe-shaped bracelets of brass or copper which were used as a form of currency, particular in the Niger delta. They were manufactured in Europe and often used as a source for metal work in Africa.

An English flintlock blunderbuss from the late eighteenth century.

Operation of the slave trade

Preparing a ship for a slave voyage was a complex and expensive business. Ships were usually fitted out by a single merchant on behalf of the owners – fellow merchants, bankers, politicians, landowners and other investors. Even people of modest means could buy a share. The average cost of fitting out a ship in 1790 was about £10,000 (approximately £550,000 today). By sharing the investment, merchants shared the risk. It also meant that they shared the profits.

The ship had to be equipped and loaded with European goods to exchange for enslaved Africans. Goods were selected to appeal to particular African slave traders and included Indian fabrics, Manchester cottons, copper and brass wear, beads, alcohol, firearms and gunpowder.

When the ship arrived at the African coast, trade was usually conducted formally at European-run forts on the African coast. Forts such as Elmina and Cape Coast Castle still stand today as reminders of the trade. Elsewhere captains negotiated directly with Africans and generally had to pay customs and dues for the right to trade.

Having exchanged their European goods for captured Africans, the slave traders sailed across the Atlantic Ocean to the Americas, where the African slaves were sold to plantation owners and other traders. Before the return journey to Europe they purchased American produce such as cotton, sugar and tobacco – the materials that slaves had laboured to produce. Once back in Europe the goods were sold and the whole process was repeated.

Africans resisted the traders who tried to take them. This image shows a group of Central African villagers shelling the slave traders' stockade using a small cannon.
© Anti-Slavery International

SHELLING THE STOCKADES OF THE SLAVERS.

Liverpool: capital of the transatlantic slave trade

Britain did not enter the slave trade until the 1650s, although Sir John Hawkins and a few others, including Sir Francis Drake, had made a dozen or so slaving voyages to Africa in the early years of Queen Elizabeth's reign in the sixteenth century.

LEFT: *A Liverpool Slave Ship* by William Jackson, 1780. It was said that the smell of vomit, urine, faeces and sweat alerted a town to the arrival of a slave ship.

The driving force behind Britain's becoming involved in the trade was the acquisition of colonies in the West Indies, and particularly Jamaica, which Britain had seized from Spain in 1655. The Caribbean sugar plantations required a huge labour force, and the Spanish were already using enslaved Africans for the work.

On 3 October 1699, Liverpool's first recorded slave ship, *Liverpool Merchant*, set sail for Africa. She eventually delivered a cargo of 220 Africans to Barbados before returning to Liverpool on 18 September 1700. In November 1699 a second slave ship, *The Blessing*, set sail for the Gold Coast of Africa.

A contemporary builders' model of the slave ship *Watt* (1797)

ABOVE: This view of Liverpool in 1725 shows the town's first dock, the customs house, the exchange and town hall.

Merchants from London and Bristol were the first Englishmen to profit on any scale from the slave trade. However, by the 1740s Liverpool merchants had overtaken them, and by 1750 Liverpool was sending forth more slave ships than Bristol and London combined. From this time onwards until the abolition of the British slave trade in 1807, Liverpool dominated the trade.

By the 1780s Liverpool was considered the European capital of the transatlantic slave trade. Vast profits from the trade helped to transform Liverpool into one of Britain's most important and wealthy cities. Other European ports such as Amsterdam, Barcelona, Bordeaux, Cadiz, Lisbon and Nantes were heavily involved too, but in total more than 5000 slave voyages were made from Liverpool, more than 3000 from London and 2000 from Bristol.

A drunken actor, George Cooke, was booed off stage in Liverpool in 1772, when he cried out: 'I have not come here to be insulted by a set of wretches, every brick in whose infernal town is cemented with an African's blood'

Thomas Golightly (1732–1821) was just one example of Liverpool's principal merchants and citizens, including many of the mayors, who were involved in the slave trade.

This eighteenth century earthenware ship bowl features the slogan 'Success to the Dobson'. The *Dobson* was a slave ship, built in Liverpool in 1770. The bowl was made to mark her launch.

'The Black Boy' in this portrait by William Windus (1844) is said to have crossed the Atlantic to Liverpool as a stowaway. Before the American Civil War, Black Americans found the idea of living in England tempting. It was a potential haven where their freedom was guaranteed. However, on arrival in England, those who managed to escape were often forced onto the streets.

A detail from the doorway of the former Martin's Bank on Water Street – the centre of commerce in Liverpool during the slaving period. Two African children are shown holding money bags and anchors.

Liverpool's orginal Town Hall was funded by local businessmen, many of whom had made their fortunes through the slave trade. As many as 16 of Liverpool's mayors are thought to have been slave merchants. Today the frieze around the outside illustrates the sources of Liverpool's wealth and African trading routes, and includes lions, crocodiles, elephants and human faces.

Reasons for Liverpool's 'success'

Overall, Liverpool was responsible for half the British slave trade, and her ships carried perhaps 1.5 million Africans into slavery. In the peak year of 1799, ships sailing from Liverpool carried more than 45,000 slaves from Africa to the Americas.

There were several reasons for the city's success in dominating the slave trade. Liverpool was reached easily by river and canal, so trade goods such as cloth, guns and iron, manufactured in enormous quantities in the Britain of the Industrial Revolution, were brought cheaply to the port.

This is a cone of sugar. Liverpool's merchants flourished by handling the sugar and other slave-produced goods brought into the city by ships returning from the Americas.

Another reason was Liverpool's merchants. They were sharp and entrepreneurial, undercutting their rivals' costs, reducing turnaround times and increasing the flexibility of operation. They developed working relationships with African traders and so knew exactly which goods the traders most wanted in exchange for a cargo of slaves.

'...the people of Liverpool, in their indiscriminate rage for commerce and getting money at all events, have nearly engrossed this Trade.'

WILLIAM MATTHEWS, BRISTOL WRITER, 1794

Founded in 1708 and built 1716–17, the Bluecoat was a school for orphans partly funded by Bryan Blundell, the merchant and trader. Blundell did not transport slaves from Africa, as commonly thought, but he did carry tobacco and other plantation goods produced by slaves.
© Arthur John Picton

'Almost every man in Liverpool is a merchant… Many of the small vessels are fitted out by attornies, drapers, ropers, grocers, tallow-chandlers, barbers, tailors.'

J. WALLACE, LIVERPOOL WRITER, 1795

Penrhyn Castle in North Wales was built on the profits of a Jamaican sugar plantation. © The Ancient Brit/Flickr

Economic benefits of slavery

The profits from slavery helped change the industrial and economic landscape of Britain and other parts of Western Europe. As the transatlantic slave trade was growing, Britain was transformed into the First Industrial Nation.

Successful slave owners amassed huge fortunes. This wealth was used to build grand houses and to invest in other enterprises such as iron, coal and banking. Penrhyn Castle in North Wales was built with the profits from a Jamaican sugar plantation, while Richard Watt purchased Speke Hall in Liverpool with the money made from the same trade. Liverpool Town Hall was funded by local businessmen, many of whom had made their fortunes through the slave trade. Today the frieze around the outside of the building illustrates Liverpool's African trading links and features lions, crocodiles, elephants and human faces.

Britain's economy was changed by the increased demand for plantation produce. Even the working classes could afford to consume sugar on a regular basis: it was no longer a luxury. The cotton industry powered technological innovation and industrial development, speeding up the process of turning this raw material into finished goods.

As the demand for plantation produce increased, so did the demand for enslaved Africans to produce it.

In order to purchase more Africans, British traders needed more trade goods – guns, textiles, and luxury goods. The flow of goods to ports like Liverpool increased to such an extent that rivers were made more navigable and canals and roads were constructed.

This seal shows King George III's coat of arms and the words 'OFFICE FOR REGISTRATION OF SLAVES DEMERARY'.
It demonstrates the extent to which slavery was a state-sanctioned trade.

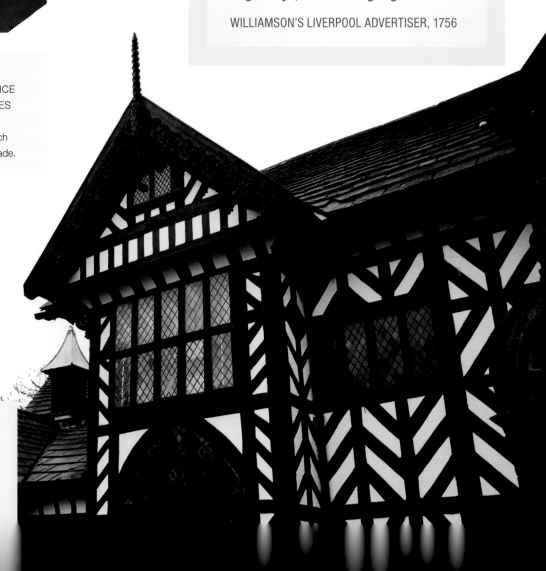

Speke Hall in Liverpool was the home of Richard Watt, a local merchant who bought the house with the profits from his sugar plantations in Jamaica.
© Etrusia UK/Flickr

Tropical goods and the rise of the consumer society

The transatlantic slave trade and the products of slave labour fed the development of consumerism in Europe.

It became common for people to wear clothes made from American cotton and coloured with American dyes. They smoked pipes filled with Virginian tobacco while drinking coffee and chocolate from Cuba and Brazil. They ate food and drink sweetened with Caribbean sugar while sitting on mahogany chairs at mahogany tables from the Caribbean and Central America. All of these goods were the products of slave labour.

It was not just the materials they produced, but the enslaved Africans themselves who became part of this consumerism. Wealthy English families showed off their Black servants, evidence of their great wealth and social standing. Enslaved Africans became exotic accessories and would often be dressed exquisitely to reflect the riches of their masters. However, their fine clothes hid the reality that Black servants were often brutally treated and were essentially slaves.

'I saw numbers of fellow beings regularly bartered for gold and transferred like cattle, or any common merchandise, from one possessor to another.'

GEORGE PINCKARD, ARMY PHYSICIAN, BARBADOS, 1796

This portrait of *The Family of Sir William Young* by Johan Zoffany features a Black servant. He is included in the painting not because he was 'one of the family' but to show the family's wealth.

REE PIAZZAS

CREAT NEWTON STREET L3

[TARLETON STREET]   [CUNLIFFE STREET]

[RODNEY STREET]   [EARLE STREET]

[GOREE PIAZZAS]   [PENNY LANE]

[Gt NEWTON STREET]   [JAMAICA STREET]

Several Liverpool streets are named after local merchants who were involved in slavery and related trades, including the world famous Penny Lane.
Photograph: Lee Garland. © National Museums Liverpool/Redman Design

Enslavement and the Middle Passage

'He took a limb of a tree that had two prongs, and shaped it so that it would cross the back of my neck, it was then fastened in front with an iron bolt; the stick was about six feet long.'

BAQUAQUA, FORMER SLAVE, 1854

Separation, trauma, desperation and loss were the fate of those Africans who were forcibly uprooted and enslaved.

Slave traders raided far inland from the coast to find their victims, whether men, women or children. After capture, Africans were shackled together and held in atrocious, dehumanising conditions. The long journey from the African interior to the sea was so difficult, often hundreds of miles, that possibly half of all kidnapped Africans died before even being loaded onto a slave ship. Sold perhaps several times on this journey, they passed from one owner to another, their sense of disorientation and dread heightening with each sale. This journey may have taken six weeks or more.

The message when the enslaved Africans eventually reached the coastal holding forts was clear: the impaled skeletons of those who had tried to run away remained as gruesome warnings to deter escape.

dis poem
shall speak of the wretched sea
that washed ships to these shores
of mothers cryin for their
young swallowed up by the sea.

MUTABARUKA, POET, 1992

This iron slave coffle dates from around 1800. It was used to secure enslaved Africans in a chain gang as they were marched to the African coast for transfer to the Americas.

Cape Coast Castle in Ghana was built for the timber and gold trades, but became one of several holding forts for the transatlantic slave trade.

Caravans of African slaves were marched from
inland areas to the African coast for sale. They
were often tethered by wooden yokes and chains
to prevent escape.
© Anti-Slavery International

DESCRIPTION OF A SLAVE SHIP.

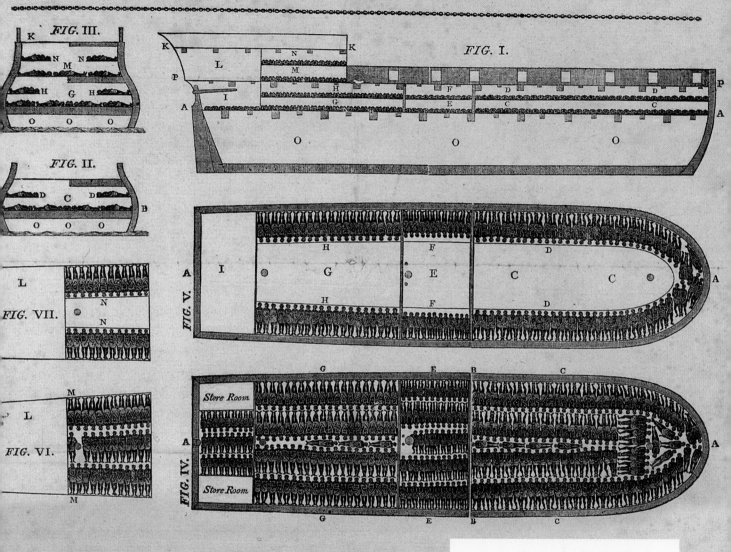

The Middle Passage:
voyage through death

The term 'Middle Passage' refers to the transporting of enslaved Africans across the Atlantic Ocean from Africa to the Americas. Over a 400-year period, the Middle Passage came to represent all of the brutality and trauma suffered by enslaved Africans.

After a holding period at a coastal fort, the enslaved Africans were delivered to the slave ships. Violence, terror and degradation were everyday occurrences on board. The Africans were branded with hot irons and restrained with shackles. They were packed in hot, cramped and suffocating conditions in the hold, with men kept separate from women and children. In good weather they were brought on deck, where they were often humiliated and forced to 'dance' for the crew. Women especially were violently abused and rape was common.

The physical conditions, fear and uncertainty left many Africans totally traumatised and unable to eat. Some preferred death and tried to take their own lives – not all were successful. There were revolts on one in ten transatlantic slave voyages, mostly while the ship was still close to the African coast. There were few successes, though, with most on-board revolts being put down with brutal ferocity.

Disease and violence also took their toll. Between 10 and 25% of the Africans died on each journey. The 1789 British Privy Council Enquiry gave 12.5% as the figure. By any measure, this was an appalling mortality rate.

'I imagine there can be but one place more horrible in all creation than the hold of a slave ship, and that place is where slaveholders are the most likely to find themselves one day.'

BAQUAQUA, FORMER SLAVE, 1854

These leg irons date from the eighteenth century. They prevented movement, possibly on board ships and while waiting to board.

Impact on Africa

The transatlantic slave trade operated for almost 400 years, and in that time at least 12 million Africans were transported forcibly. However, many millions more were affected profoundly by the trade.

Two thirds of enslaved Africans were males aged between 15 and 25. By stealing away their young people, the trade robbed the African workforce of young and healthy individuals, causing industrial and economic stagnation. Agriculture suffered as fertile land was abandoned by those fleeing from European slavers. Successful trade routes that had existed long before European intervention were disrupted. Arms and ammunition brought to Africa by European traders helped perpetuate conflict and political instability. The transatlantic slave trade distorted African societies, and the development of African communities and cultures was severely stunted as a result.

The labour and inventiveness that should have shaped the African homeland were instead used to transform the Americas and enrich Western Europe.

'...the whites are dragging us around in chains and in handcuffs, to their new States and Territories to work their mines and farms, to enrich them and their children.'

DAVID WALKER, POLITICAL ACTIVIST, 1829

This Ghanaian brass figure was used to weigh the gold which was central to the Asante economy. The brass was mainly imported from Europe, and the shapes (in this case a man with a gun) show European influences.

These wrought iron shackles comprise a neck iron and chains. They were mainly used to restrain male slaves, who made up two thirds of those taken.

Africans tried to defend their villages from armed slave traders, but often could not match their firepower or were caught unawares.

© Anti-Slavery International

Life and death in the Americas

'A slave must move by the will of another, hence the necessity of terror to coerce his obedience.'

JAMAICAN PLANTATION OWNER, 1763

Sale and 'seasoning'

Only a fraction, perhaps 5%, of the enslaved Africans who survived the journey to the New World ended up in British North America. The vast majority were shipped to the Caribbean sugar colonies, Brazil or Spanish America. Even so, by the 1680s, enslaved Africans were being imported to English colonies in huge numbers.

On arrival in the Americas the disoriented and frightened Africans were prepared for sale like animals. They were washed, shaved and their skin oiled to make them appear healthy and to increase their sale price.

Depending on their destination, they were sold through agents, by public auction or by a 'scramble' in which buyers simply grabbed whomever they wanted. Buyers wanted to know exactly what they were buying, and sales often involved measuring, intrusive physical examinations and branding.

This was a highly traumatic time for the new arrivals. Families and friends who had managed to stay together through the Middle Passage were now often separated forever. Frequently sold on several times, the Africans were moved from place to place, enduring the trauma of many separations, before reaching their final destination.

Negroes just landed from a Slave Ship.

This 1808 engraving shows slaves arriving in the Americas. Plantation owner Thomas Thistlewood reported that he would 'choose men-boys and girls, none exceeding 16 or 18 years old, as full grown men or women seldom turn out well; and besides, they shave the men so close and gloss them over so much that a person cannot be certain he does not buy old Negroes'.

This ivory trade token is inscribed 'Tom Buck of Granny Bonny, an Honest Trader…' These were probably exchanged as pledges or receipts.

Copy

Sales of 268 Negro Slaves imported in the Ship African ptain Thomas Trader from Malemba on the Acct & Risque Messrs John Cole and Co Owners of the said Ship. Merchants in Liverpool

To whom sold	Men	Women	Boys	Girls	Total	Price £ S D		
By James Fisher			1		1	35	—	—
John Miller			1		1	35	—	—
Augustus Valette			1		1	40	—	—
George Richards			1		1	35	—	—
Ditto			1		1	35	—	—
Papley & Wade	103	26	67	34	230 @	7820	—	—
Chambers & Mead	5		2	1	8 @	296	—	—
Sloop Two Brothers			6		6 @	204	—	—
Mons. Fontanelle				2	2 @ 36£	72	—	—
John Darcy			2		2 @ 30£ msg.	60	—	—
Ditto	4	3	2	3	12 @ 35£	420	—	—
Alexan Forceston		1		1	2 Sickly	30	—	—
Sold at Vendue			1		1 Capt to acct for			
	112	30	85	41	268	9082	—	—

Charges Viz.t

	£ S D
To Cash paid Import Duty on 268 Slaves @ 19/8 Bond 5/-	134.5.0
To Ditto paid the Boatler his head money on ditto @ 1/2	13.8.-
To Ditto paid Captain Trader his Coast Commiss" @ 4£ p 104 on 9082£ Gross Sales	349.6.2
To my Commission @ 5£ p Cent on the Gross Sales	454.2.-
	951 1 2
	8130 18 10

To Messrs John Cole & Co. Owners of the African in Acct Curr for nt

Errors Excepted
Kingston Jamaica 19th Sept 1764
℘ Wm Boyd —

'The devil was in the Englishman, that he makes everything work; he makes the Negro work, the horse work, the ass work, the wood work, and the wind work.'

GREAT NEWS FROM BARBADOS, OR A TRUE AND FAITHFUL ACCOUNT OF THE GRAND CONSPIRACY OF NEGROES AGAINST THE ENGLISH, 1676

Sold, branded and issued with a new name, the Africans were separated from family and friends and stripped of their identity. In a deliberate process which aimed to break their willpower and leave them passive and subservient, enslaved Africans were 'seasoned'. For a period of two or three years they were 'trained' to obey or receive the lash, and acclimatised to their work and conditions. Here was mental and physical torture. A quarter of the Africans who had survived the long journey to the African coast and then the Middle Passage now died during this period. Some took their own lives. Some ran away and joined communities of 'maroons' (see p. 57).

Those who survived somehow found ways to endure. They could not escape. There was no hope for them, for their children, their grandchildren, or even their great grandchildren. Slavery was, as far as anyone knew, a nightmare that would never end.

TOP LEFT: Slaves were branded to show they were property and considered little more than animals.
Photograph: Lee Garland. © National Museums Liverpool/Redman Design

BOTTOM LEFT: This list describes the sale of 268 slaves imported into Jamaica on the Liverpool ship *African* in September 1794. The sale of the Africans raised over £9,000.

between the Hours of 11 o'Clock in the Forenoon and One o'Clock in the Afternoon, on the Estate of *Gavin Hamilton*, Esq. in the Parish of *St. David*, will be sold to the highest Bidder for ready Gold and Silver Money, all the Right and Title of *John Edward Hamilton*, Esq. to a Bull, an Ox, a Cow and a Ram Sheep, (which were before advertised, but could not then be come at) levied on by Virtue of sundry Executions, and will be sold as aforesaid, unless in the mean Time the Plaintiffs are paid their Debts and Costs.

JOHN HORNE, Dep. Prov. Mar.

WHEREAS a Negro Woman Slave, named ROSE, well known in this Island, the Property of Mr. *David Kidd*, who has for some Time past absconded from his Service, did this Day in Mr. *Kidd's* Absence from the Island, in a felonious manner enter into his House and take therefrom sundry Articles. This is to give Notice, That if any Person or Persons shall apprehend the said Negro Woman ROSE, and deliver her to the Subscriber in *Kingstown*, he or they shall be handsomely rewarded.---- And all Persons are requested not to harbour her, as they will answer it at their Peril.

JOSEPH FRASER.

Kingstown, Oct. 3, 1789.

Marshal's Office, St. Vincent, September 15, 1789.
NOTICE IS HEREBY GIVEN, That on *Saturday* the 24th Day of *October* next, between the Hours of Eleven o'Clock in the Forenoon, and One o'Clock in the Afternoon, and the Hour of Four o'Clock in the Afternoon and the setting of

A newspaper cutting seeking Rose, a runaway slave. From the *Royal St Vincent Gazette & General Advertiser*, Saturday 10 October 1789.

Chattel slavery

'I appear before this immense assembly as a thief and a robber. I stole this head, these limbs, this body from my master and ran off with them.'

FREDERICK DOUGLASS, FORMER SLAVE AND ABOLITION CAMPAIGNER, 1853

'Chattel' is an old word for property. Chattel slavery was far worse than any form of slavery that had previously existed in Europe or Africa.

Enslaved Africans, and the children they bore, became chattel slaves, which meant that they were the outright property of their masters. They were regarded simply as commodities, without human rights, and were exposed to the most ruthless abuse and crippling workload. Such atrocities went unchallenged because chattel slaves had no right to complain.

Shackles allowed slave traders to control many slaves at the same time.

Chattel slaves were bought and sold like animals, as this sale advertisement shows.

Africans were branded with hot irons, like cattle, to mark them out as possessions. The plantation owners and slave traders alike justified their atrocious actions by claiming that Black men, women and children were closer to animals than they were to white people, and so should be treated as such.

Sale of Slaves and Stock.

The Negroes and Stock listed below, are a Prime Lot, and belong to the ESTATE OF THE LATE LUTHER McGOWAN, and will be sold on Monday, Sept. 22nd, 1852, at the Fair Grounds, in Savannah, Georgia, at 1:00 P. M. The Negroes will be taken to the grounds two days previous to the Sale, so that they may be inspected by prospective buyers.

On account of the low prices listed below, they will be sold for cash only, and must be taken into custody within two hours after sale.

No.	Name.	Age	Remarks.	Price.
1	Lunesta	27	Prime Rice Planter,	$1,275.00
2	Violet	16	Housework and Nursemaid,	900.00
3	Lizzie	30	Rice, Unsound,	300.00
4	Minda	27	Cotton, Prime Woman,	1,200.00
5	Adam	28	Cotton, Prime Young Man,	1,100.00
6	Abel	41	Rice Hand, Eyesight Poor,	675.00
7	Tanney	22	Prime Cotton Hand,	950.00
8	Flementina	39	Good Cook, Stiff Knee,	400.00
9	Lanney	34	Prime Cottom Man,	1,000.00
10	Sally	10	Handy in Kitchen,	675.00
11	Maccabey	35	Prime Man, Fair Carpenter,	980.00
12	Dorcas Judy	25	Seamstress, Handy in House,	800.00
13	Happy	60	Blacksmith,	575.00
14	Mowden	15	Prime Cotton Boy,	700.00
15	Bills	21	Handy with Mules,	900.00
16	Theopolis	39	Rice Hand, Gets Fits,	575.00
17	Coolidge	29	Rice Hand and Blacksmith,	1,275.00
18	Bessie	69	Infirm, Sews,	250.00
19	Infant	1	Strong Likely Boy	400.00
20	Samson	41	Prime Man, Good with Stock,	975.00
21	Callie May	27	Prime Woman, Rice,	1,000.00
22	Honey	14	Prime Girl, Hearing Poor,	850.00
23	Angelina	16	Prime Girl, House or Field,	1,000.00
24	Virgil	21	Prime Field Hand,	1,100.00
25	Tom	40	Rice Hand, Lame Leg,	750.00
26	Noble	11	Handy Boy,	900.00
27	Judge Lesh	55	Prime Blacksmith,	800.00
28	Booster	43	Fair Mason, Unsound,	600.00
29	Big Kate	37	Housekeeper and Nurse,	950.00
30	Melie Ann	19	Housework, Smart Yellow Girl,	1,250.00
31	Deacon	26	Prime Rice Hand,	1,000.00
32	Coming	19	Prime Cotton Hand,	1,000.00
33	Mabel	47	Prime Cotton Hand,	800.00
34	Uncle Tim	60	Fair Hand with Mules,	600.00
35	Abe	27	Prime Cotton Hand,	1,000.00
36	Tennes	29	Prime Rice Hand and Cocahman,	1,250.00

There will also be offered at this sale, twenty head of Horses and Mules with harness, along with thirty head of Prime Cattle. Slaves will be sold separate, or in lots, as best suits the purchaser. Sale will be held rain or shine.

Plantation life

'The conch shell blowed afore daylight and all hands better git out for roll call or Solomon bust the door down and get them out. It was work hard, git beatins and half fed.'

MARY REYNOLDS, FORMER SLAVE, 1936

The stark reality of plantation life was one of never-ending brutality and forced labour. The treatment of slaves was harsh and inhumane. Whether labouring or simply walking about in public, people living as slaves were regulated by legally authorised violence. According to an account by a plantation overseer to a visitor: 'some negroes are determined never to let a white man whip them and will resist you, when you attempt it; of course you must kill them in that case'.

As well as physical abuse and murder, slaves were at constant risk of losing members of their families if their owners decided to trade them for profit, punishment, or to pay debts.

Slaves were provided with minimal food, clothing, housing and medical care. In many households, a slave's treatment varied with the colour of their skin. Darker-skinned slaves worked in the fields, while lighter-skinned house servants had comparatively better clothing, food and housing.

Slaves were considered legal non-persons except if they committed crimes. An Alabama court asserted that slaves

This engraving shows a Brazilian sugar plantation. These were brutal places where a slave's life expectancy was low. As well as disease and killings, there were many accidents involving machinery and tools that resulted in mutilations and sometimes death.

'...are rational beings, they are capable of committing crimes; and in reference to acts which are crimes, are regarded as persons. Because they are slaves, they are incapable of performing civil acts, and, in reference to all such, they are things, not persons.'

Sugar is relatively easy to grow. Stalks from mature sugar canes were buried in shallow holes and were ready for harvesting within 15 months.

This engine and crushing mill was used to crush the sugar cane to release the sap within. It was made by Fletcher and Co. of London and Derby, and is still in place at New River, Nevis. © Rob Philpott

Flagellation of a Female Samboe Slave.

Blake Sculpt.

A model of a sugar plantation, on display in the International Slavery Museum.

Photograph: Lee Garland. © National Museums Liverpool/Redman Design

Pioneers of the Americas

'We have been a source of wealth to this Republic… Our tears and blood were sacrificed at the altar of this nation's avarice. Our unpaid labour was a stepping stone to its financial success.'

SOJOURNER TRUTH, FORMER SLAVE AND ABOLITION CAMPAIGNER, 1875

The forced labour of millions of enslaved Africans and their descendants transformed the landscape and future of the Americas.

They cleared forests, built roads and houses, dug canals, and worked down mines, all to the financial benefit of their owners. They grew produce such as sugar, cotton and tobacco, and created the wealth that supported the plantation owners and their families.

The Africans were, though, not just a source of labour. They brought a wide range of skills to the Americas, such as rice-growing and metal-working. Many owners hired out their skilled slaves to work for other masters, especially in the growing towns and cities that needed a skilled workforce.

The labour of Africans helped transform the landscape and industry across the Americas. Their efforts should have been benefiting Africa.

I SELL THE SHADOW TO SUPPORT THE SUBSTANCE.

SOJOURNER TRUTH.

Sojourner Truth was a former slave, abolitionist, preacher and advocate of women's rights.
Courtesy of the Library of Congress, LC-USZ62-119343

Resistance

Africans did not simply accept their slavery, but instead fought against their oppressors in numerous ways. There were uprisings and rebellions as well as other less obvious methods of resistance. Slaves stole from their owners, damaged machinery, worked slowly and pretended to be sick.

One famous example of resistance in the Southern United States was Nat Turner's Rebellion in Virginia in August 1831. Turner was an enslaved American-born man who had lived his entire life in Southampton County, Virginia. He led a group of rebel slaves from house to house, freeing slaves and killing about 55 white people. This was the highest number of deaths caused by any slave uprising in the South. The rebellion was put down within a few days, though Turner survived in hiding for several months before being captured and arrested. On 5 November 1831, Turner was tried, convicted and sentenced to death. He was hanged in Jerusalem, Virginia. Those who resisted slavery were brave individuals because all acts of resistance, no matter how small, carried the threat of severe and inhumane punishment if discovered.

An eighteenth century Caribbean newspaper advert, looking for news of Jacob, a runaway slave. Most runaway slaves were recaptured – their skin colour made them stand out – but some were helped to evade capture.

LEFT: The slave trade was abolished in Britain in 1807 but full emancipation was not achieved in British territories until 1834 and 1862 in the United States. Painted in 1861, the year of the outbreak of the American Civil War, *The Hunted Slaves* by Richard Andsell portrays two runaway slaves and is a powerful indictment of the savage treatment slaves suffered.

This eighteenth century iron punishment collar was just one of several designs. Some prevented slaves from sleeping, others from eating or talking.

Harriet Tubman was a remarkable woman. Born into slavery, she later escaped and became a 'conductor' on the Underground Railroad, leading more than 300 escaped slaves to freedom. During the American Civil War she became the first US woman to plan and lead a military expedition, which freed more than 700 slaves.

Courtesy of the Library of Congress, LC-USZ62-7816

'Slavery broke the world in half, it broke it in every way. It broke Europe. It made them into something else. It made them crazy. You can't do that for hundreds of years and it not take a toll.'

TONI MORRISON, WRITER, 1988

Harriet Tubman (1823 – 1913)
nurse, spy and scout

'A female negro slave, with a weight chained to her ankle'.
Means of restraint were often cumbersome and cruel.

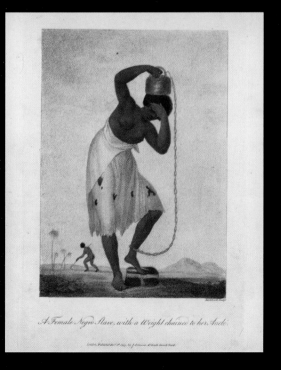

Diane Nash was instrumental in the birth and development of America's Civil Rights Movement. She is shown here speaking at the International Slavery Museum.

M Rainsford del.   Barlow sculp.

*Revenge taken by the Black Army for the Cruelties practised
on them by the French.*

The image shows the 'Black Army' carrying out revenge hangings of French military officers during the Haitian Revolution (1791–1804). The war was fought between colonialists and their Haitian slaves, and led to Haiti becoming a free republic.

Maroons

Groups of runaway slaves in the Caribbean and South America became known collectively as 'maroons'. Their name comes from the Spanish word *cimarrón*, meaning 'wild' or 'untamed'. Maroons maintained their independence by a combination of guerrilla fighting, good organisation and diplomacy.

Europeans in the Caribbean were outnumbered by their slaves by about ten to one. This created a climate of fear, and, in the face of maroon wars, Carib wars and slave revolts, slave owners lived in constant fear of rebellion.

Toussaint Louverture

François-Dominique Toussaint L'Ouverture (c.1743–1803) was a former plantation slave who became an influential military leader in the Haitian Revolution.
© Anti-Slavery International

Pro-slavery arguments

In the nineteenth century, supporters of slavery often defended the institution as a 'necessary evil'. They feared that the emancipation of slaves would have more harmful social and economic consequences than the continuation of slavery. In 1820, Thomas Jefferson wrote that with slavery, 'We have the wolf by the ear, and we can neither hold him, nor safely let him go. Justice is in one scale, and self-preservation in the other.'

John C. Calhoun, in an infamous speech in the United States Senate in 1837, declared that slavery was 'instead of an evil, a good – a positive good'.

The Execution of Breaking on the Rack.

'For they cannot be justified, unless they shall be able to prove, that a Negro slave is neither man, woman nor child.'

GRANVILLE SHARP, ABOLITIONIST, 1769

The Execution of Breaking on the Rack, 1792. Slaves were often forced to inflict brutal punishments on each other. These images also reinforced European racial prejudices, viewing Africans as little more than animals.

Robert E. Lee wrote in 1856:

'There are few, I believe, in this enlightened age, who will not acknowledge that slavery as an institution is a moral and political evil. I think it is a greater evil to the white than to the colored race. While my feelings are strongly enlisted in behalf of the latter, my sympathies are more deeply engaged for the former. The blacks are immeasurably better off here than in Africa, morally, physically, and socially. The painful discipline they are undergoing is necessary for their further instruction as a race, and will prepare them, I hope, for better things.'

A Surinam Planter in his
Morning Dress. The planter
is shown being served by a
female slave.

The end of slavery

Abolition of the British slave trade

Opposition to slavery and the slave trade produced the first mass movement in British history. The campaign in Britain to end trading in enslaved Africans began in 1787 and was led in Parliament by William Wilberforce. A number of Black people were prominent in the campaign, including Olaudah Equiano and Ottobah Cuguano.

Many slave traders and plantation owners had made their fortune from the trade and opposed the campaign. There was particularly strong opposition in Liverpool. One of Wilberforce's most vocal opponents in Parliament was Banastre Tarleton, a member of one of Liverpool's leading families. The Reverend Raymond Harris (a pseudonym of the Spanish Jesuit, Raimondo Hormoza) wrote a pamphlet entitled *Scriptural Researches on the licitness of the Slave Trade* which provided biblical support for the slave trade, and for which he received a £100 reward from Liverpool Town Council.

In 1788 the list of subscribers to the Society for Abolition included just eight Liverpudlians, including William Roscoe and the Quakers William Rathbone and his son. The most outspoken critic of the slave trade was Edward Rushton, known as the blind poet, who had lost his sight from disease on the African coast and who had direct experience of the trade.

This full-sized figure dates from the late nineteenth century. It shows an enslaved African breaking free of his chains in what may be seen as a symbolic gesture. It is similar to other carved figures in the American folk art tradition.

A copper and enamel patch box, dating from 1790, with the abolitionist motif 'AM I NOT A MAN AND A BROTHER'.

William Wilberforce (1759–1833)
was an English parliamentarian
and leader of the campaign to
abolish British slavery.
© Anti-Slavery International

One of Liverpool's most experienced slavers, James Penny (who gave his name to Penny Lane in the city), received a magnificent piece of silver tableware in reward for his report to a Privy Council Committee on slavery, as well as, ironically, the Freedom of the Borough of Liverpool.

'Interest is so much blended with Humanity in this Business that… every Attention is generally paid to the Lives and Health of the Slaves.'

JAMES PENNY'S WORDS TO THE PRIVY COUNCIL COMMITTEE IN 1788

ABOVE: This abolition medal was produced to celebrate the end of slavery throughout British lands during the reign of William IV on 1 August 1834. It features psalm 118, verse 23 and reads, 'This is the Lord's doing: it is marvellous in our eyes'.

BELOW: This cup features a chained slave being whipped by an overseer, and was produced to further the abolitionists' cause.

The centrepiece presented to James Penny in 1792 by Liverpool Town Council in recognition of his support of the slave trade.

In 1806 Liverpool elected the pro-abolitionist Roscoe as a Member of Parliament. This perhaps shows that even Liverpool's voting elite recognised that the slave trade was coming to an end. The Act to abolish the British slave trade, but not slavery itself, was passed finally in March 1807.

In the following 50 years, Britain became a major campaigner to end the trade by other nations. The Royal Navy established a West Africa Squadron which seized about 1,600 slave ships and freed 150,000 Africans on board. Britain signed anti-slavery treaties with more than 50 African rulers, and action was taken against those leaders who refused to outlaw the trade.

This early nineteenth century china plate features abolitionist slogans such as, 'So Christian Light dispels the gloom, That shades poor Negro's hapless doom.'

This engraving features abolition campaigner and former slave Olaudah Equiano, and is taken from the 1793 edition of his autobiography.

William Roscoe was a historian, poet, art collector, lawyer, politician and philanthropist who worked tirelessly to abolish slavery. In 1806 he was elected as Liverpool's Member of Parliament, suggesting a change in the town's attitudes towards the trade.

Plate marking the abolition of slavery.
It reads 'Freedom First of August 1838'.

Despite the ban on British slave trading, no slave was freed in 1807. Instead, conditions worsened for slaves, provoking more revolts. In Britain, abolitionists such as Wilberforce and Roscoe continued to wage political and literary campaigns against slavery.

Slavery in the British colonies finally came to an end in 1833, with the passing of the Slavery Abolition Act. Slave owners received £20 million (around £1 billion today) in compensation from the British government. Freed slaves received nothing.

At least 12 million Africans were enslaved over a period of 400 years before transatlantic slavery was finally ended.

Freedom in the Americas

Slavery was gradually abolished in the Northern United States, with all Northern states passing emancipation acts between 1777 and 1804. For the slave owners of the Southern states, though, emancipation was unthinkable. This issue was one of the prime causes of the American Civil War, and in 1860 the Southern states broke away from the Union to form the Confederate States of America.

When the American Civil War ended in 1865 with the defeat of the Confederate States, the United States government abolished slavery. Legally, the last 40,000 or so slaves were freed in Kentucky by the final ratification of the Thirteenth Amendment to the Constitution in December 1865. Slaves still held in New Jersey, Delaware, West Virginia, Maryland, Missouri and Washington DC also became legally free on this date.

Elsewhere, Portugal abolished slavery in 1869, while Brazil did not end slavery until 1888.

The crew of the *CSS Alabama* are shown in Cape Town, South Africa, in August 1863. The ship was a Confederate blockade runner during the American Civil War.

Many Liverpool merchants supported the Confederate States in the American Civil War, having made their fortunes from the slave trade. Built in 1863 in Liverpool, the *PS Banshee* was the first of the so-called 'blockade runners' commissioned by the South to beat the blockade imposed by the Federal Navy during the war. This painting is by Samuel Walters.

'My paramount object in this struggle is to save the Union, and is not either to save or to destroy slavery. If I could save the Union without freeing any slave I would do it, and if I could save it by freeing all the slaves I would do it; and if I could save it by freeing some and leaving others alone I would also do that. What I do about slavery, and the colored race, I do because I believe it helps to save the Union... I have here stated my purpose according to my view of official duty; and I intend no modification of my oft-expressed personal wish that all men everywhere could be free.'

ABRAHAM LINCOLN IN A LETTER TO HORACE GREELEY, EDITOR OF THE *NEW YORK TRIBUNE*, 22 AUGUST 1862

Frederick Douglass was born a slave but rose to become a leader of the abolitionist movement and advisor to Abraham Lincoln.
Courtesy of the Library of Congress, LC-USZ62-15887

This American electoral tally reads 'Millions for freedom. Not one cent for slavery' and 'Success to Republican principles'.

The legacy of slavery

Racism

Transatlantic slavery has left an extremely damaging and dangerous legacy of racism. Attempts to legitimise and justify slavery – seeing African culture as inferior to European civilisation – contributed to the spread of modern racism.

The idea of white supremacy grew out of transatlantic slavery. The fact that Africans were Black made it possible to defend their enslavement in terms of the colour of their skin, and slave owners justified their abuse and violence towards enslaved Africans by claiming that they were inferior to whites. The laws that these white supremacists created denied enslaved Africans the most basic human rights, and laid the foundations for modern racism in Western society.

Many people are negative about others because they have been conditioned by society to adopt racist ideologies. Racism is regarded by all – except racists – as totally unacceptable, and a violation of human rights.

> '**I ain't got no quarrel with them Viet Cong… They never called me nigger.**'
>
> MUHAMMAD ALI, WORLD HEAVYWEIGHT BOXING CHAMPION, 1966

This new year's card is an example of the representation of Black people through racial stereotypes.

> '**I am going into this fight for the sole purpose of proving that a white man is better than a Negro.**'
>
> JAMES J. JEFFRIES, WHITE, PREVIOUSLY UNDEFEATED WORLD HEAVYWEIGHT BOXING CHAMPION, SHORTLY BEFORE LOSING A WORLD TITLE FIGHT TO BLACK TITLEHOLDER JACK JOHNSON, 1910

The fight for civil rights

In the last 150 years the struggle for equality and civil rights has continued. In the United States the abolition of slavery did not lead to equality for people of African descent. On the contrary, freed slaves were treated as second-class citizens.

For decades after their emancipation, many former slaves living in the South sharecropped (giving a share of the crops raised to the landlord in lieu of rent), had a low standard of living, and suffered from discrimination through segregation, as well as violence from extremists such as the members of the Ku Klux Klan. In some states, it was only after the Civil Rights Movement of the 1950s and 1960s that Black people obtained legal protection from racial discrimination.

The Civil Rights Movement in the USA (1955–68) confronted racial discrimination and violence against African Americans. Their methods included litigation and lobbying by organisations such as the National Association for the Advancement of Colored People (NAACP).

Frustrated by lack of real progress in civil rights, African American activists adopted a strategy of non-violent resistance known as 'civil disobedience'. Organisations such as the Black Panthers, which emerged during the 1960s, adopted a more direct approach. They encouraged a new racial consciousness among Black Americans through a philosophy of 'by any means necessary'.

Even today freedom from cultural and economic oppression is not yet universally realised in the United States, and anti-racist campaigners are still inspired by the words and deeds of people such as Martin Luther King, Malcolm X and Rosa Parks.

'I have a dream that my four little children will one day live in a nation where they will not be judged by the colour of their skin, but by the content of their character. I have a dream that one day on the red hills of Georgia the sons of former slaves and the sons of former slave owners will be able to sit down together at a table of brotherhood.'

MARTIN LUTHER KING, CIVIL RIGHTS CAMPAIGNER, 1963

'The common goal of 22 million Afro-Americans is respect as human beings, the God-given right to be a human being.'

MALCOLM X, POLITICAL ACTIVIST, 1964

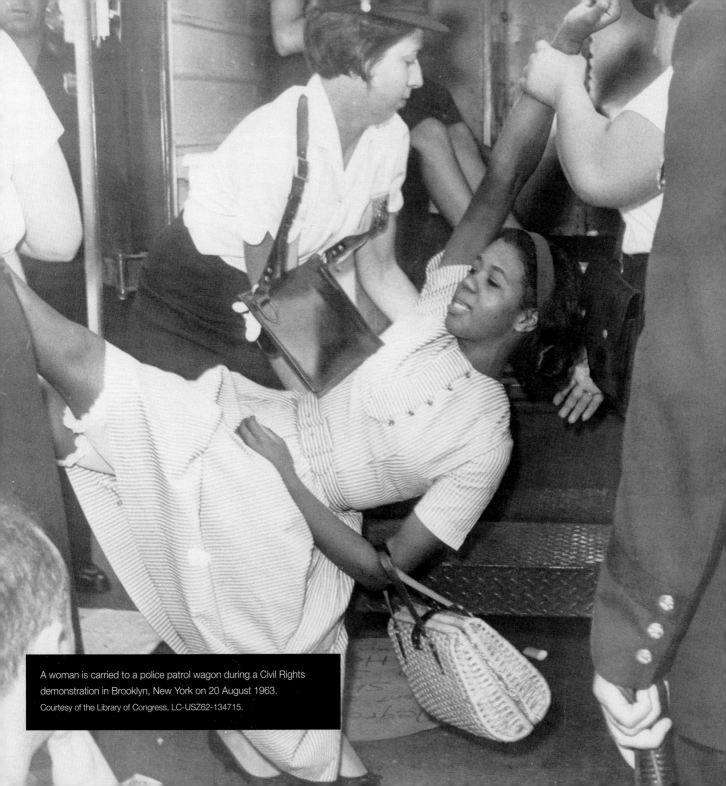

A woman is carried to a police patrol wagon during a Civil Rights demonstration in Brooklyn, New York on 20 August 1963.

Courtesy of the Library of Congress, LC-USZ62-134715.

Martin Luther King Jr was a clergyman, Nobel Peace Prize winner and one of the main leaders of the Civil Rights Movement in the United States. He adopted non-violent direct action based on the teachings of Gandhi.

"Human rights are something you were born with. Human rights are your God-given rights. Human rights are the rights that are recognized by all nations of this earth."
Malcolm X.

Courtesy of the Library of Congress, LC-U9-11695-5

In *Boarding a Slaver*, L Burke shows *USS Saratoga* about to board the American clipper *Nightingale*, which was correctly suspected of being involved in the illegal slave trade. The slave trade was abolished in the United States from 1 January 1808. However, some slaving continued on an illegal basis for the next fifty years.

'Let freedom ring. And when this happens…we will be able to speed up that day when all of God's children – Black men and white men, Jews and Gentiles, Protestants and Catholics – will be able to join hands and sing in the words of the old Negro spiritual: "Free at last! Free at last! Thank God Almighty, we are free at last!"'

MARTIN LUTHER KING, CIVIL RIGHTS CAMPAIGNER, 1963

RIGHT: The Ku Klux Klan is an overtly racist group which acts to maintain the 'supremacy' of the white race over Black people. At its height in the 1920s the Ku Klux Klan was responsible for lynching innocent Black men, women and children, even going so far as to murder uniformed Black soldiers returning from the First World War. This outfit is from Orange County, New York, and can be seen in the Legacy gallery in the International Slavery Museum.

Global inequalities

European exploitation of the Americas and Africa laid the foundation for many modern global inequalities. It has affected the development of all the countries involved, with many African, Caribbean and South American countries facing abject poverty and long-term underdevelopment as a result of slavery and colonialism.

It is no coincidence that the poorest, least developed countries today are those whose peoples were misused and manipulated over the last three centuries.

The Freedom! sculpture was commissioned by Christian Aid and National Museums Liverpool to mark the 200th anniversary of the abolition of the British slave trade in 2007. It is made out of recycled objects such as metal car parts and raw junk found in the streets of the Haitian capital, Port-au-Prince, and was created by young Haitians and sculptors.

This ankle bracelet was 'worn' by a modern-day domestic slave girl in Niger. Slavery is still a reality for millions of people across the world.

English anti-slavery campaigners pack out a theatre in Hull for a campaign meeting in 1925. A banner above the audience reads: 'Slavery, the Unspeakable Insult to God'.

© Anti-Slavery International

By the end of the nineteenth century, while the stealing of African youth through the slave trade had ended, a different type of exploitation had arrived – colonialism. The 'Great Powers' of Western Europe claimed and conquered most of Africa and carved up the continent into colonies in the 'Scramble for Africa'. Henceforth Africa's resources, like its people before, were developed and exploited by the Western European nations for their own benefit. By 1912 only Liberia and Ethiopia survived as independent African states.

Since colonialism

Colonial rule by Europeans continued until the end of the Second World War, after which the major European powers were left weakened. Thereafter, independence movements in Africa gained momentum. In 1951 Libya, a former Italian colony, gained independence. In 1956, Tunisia and Morocco won their independence from France, and Ghana followed suit in 1957.

Most of the rest of the continent became independent over the next decade, though in some countries, notably Algeria, it came only after a violent struggle. Though South Africa was one of the first African countries to gain independence, it remained under the rule of its white settler population, in a policy known as Apartheid, until 1994.

Two slaves tap rubber trees for latex on a colonial plantation in the Congo Free State (now Democratic Republic of Congo) in around 1905.
© Anti-Slavery International

Child domestic workers in modern day Benin.
© Anti-Slavery International

NATIVES COLLECTING RUBBER, LUSAMBO,

Four Angolan indentured workers (basically slaves) on the coffee or cocoa plantations of São Tomé, a Portuguese colony until 1975.
© Anti-Slavery International

These chained women were taken hostage by sentries of the Anglo-Belgian India Rubber company (ABIR) after their husbands fled into the forest to escape slavery. Congo Free State (now Democratic Republic of Congo) in around 1905.
© Anti-Slavery International

A 1923 Christmas photograph of staff at the African Oil Nuts Company and Miller Brothers in Badagry, Nigeria. The African workers were made to pose for the camera, each man's chest painted with a letter to spell out '1923, Badagry, Merry Xmas'.

© Image of Empire

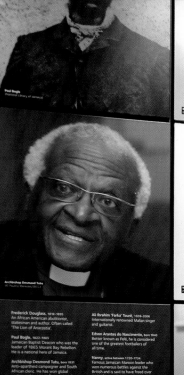

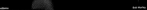

Frederick Douglass, 1818-1895
An African American abolitionist, statesman and author. Often called 'The Lion of Anacostia'.

Paul Bogle, 1822-1865
Jamaican Baptist Deacon who was the leader of 1865 Morant Bay Rebellion. He is a national hero of Jamaica.

Archbishop Desmond Tutu, born 1931
Anti-apartheid campaigner and South African cleric. He has won global acclaim in his pursuit for peace and reconciliation.

Sam Sharpe, 1801-1832
He instigated a slave revolt on Jamaica called the Christmas Rebellion in 1831. He is a national hero of Jamaica.

Susana Baca de la Colina,
Celebrated Afro-Peruvian singer who has spearheaded a resurgence and appreciation in Afro-Peruvian music.

Ali Ibrahim 'Farka' Touré, 1939-2006
Internationally renowned Malian singer and guitarist.

Edson Arantes do Nascimento, born 1940
Better known as Pelé, he is considered one of the greatest footballers of all time.

Nanny, active between 1720-1734
Famous Jamaican Maroon leader who won numerous battles against the British and is said to have freed over 800 Africans. She is a national heroine of Jamaica.

Dr Roi Ankhkara Kwabena, born 1956
Trinidadian cultural anthropologist who has worked throughout Europe, Africa, Latin-America and the Caribbean.

Viv Anderson, born 1956
The first Black England international professional footballer to play in a full match.

Lewis Howard Latimer, 1848-1928
An African American inventor who improved the use of carbon filaments in light bulbs.

Oprah Winfrey, born 1954
African American media tycoon, actor and successful business woman.

C.L.R. James, 1901-1989
Trinidadian writer, journalist and Marxist. His book 'The Black Jacobins' is considered a seminal anti-colonial work.

Pastinha Mestre 1889-1981
A mestre, or master, of the Afro-Brazilian martial art of Capoeira.

Bob Marley, 1945-1981
Internationally acclaimed reggae artist and devout Rastafarian. Many Rastafarians regard him as a prophet.

Kwame Nkrumah, 1909-1972
First president of modern Ghana and influential Pan-Africanist. He was a global campaigner against colonialism and imperialism.

Stokely Carmichael, 1941-1998
Trinidadian-American Pan-Africanist, leader of the Student Nonviolent Coordinating Committee and one time Prime Minister of the Black Panther Party.

Arthur Wharton, 1865-1930
In 2003 he was inducted into the English Football Hall of Fame for his contribution as the first Black professional football association player.

Nelson Mandela, born 1918
First fully democratically elected president of South Africa. He was leader of the African National Congress and anti-apartheid activist. He spent 27 years in prison for his beliefs.

Bessie Smith, 1892-1937
Influential and successful blues singer. Many popular musicians and singers site her as an inspiration.

Benedita Souza da Silva Sampaio, born 1942
A successful Afro-Brazilian politician who has overcome prejudice to become the Governor of the State of Rio de Janeiro and Minister of State in the government of Luiz Inacio Lula da Silva.

John Richard Archer, 1863-1932
Born in Liverpool in 1913 he became the first person of African descent to become a mayor in the UK, at Battersea. He campaigned for equality throughout his life.

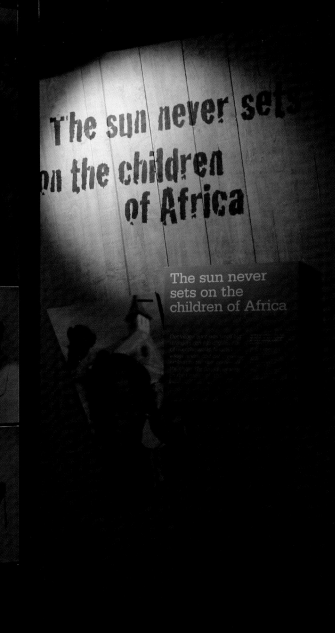

The sun never sets on the children of Africa

The Black Achievers Wall in the International Slavery Museum is a celebration of Black Achievers past and present.

Photograph: Lee Garland. © National Museums Liverpool/Redman Design

Today, Africa contains 53 independent and sovereign countries, most of which still have the borders drawn during the era of European colonialism. Since colonialism, African states have frequently been hampered by instability, corruption, violence and authoritarianism. The vast majority of African nations are republics that operate under some form of presidential system of rule. However, few of them have been able to sustain democratic governments, and many have instead experienced a series of coups, producing military dictatorships. For political gain, many African leaders have fanned ethnic conflicts that had been exacerbated, or even created, by colonial rule.

In many countries, the military was perceived as being the only group that could effectively maintain order, and many nations in Africa were under military rule during the 1970s and early 1980s. During the period from the early 1960s to the late 1980s, Africa experienced more than 70 coups and 13 presidential assassinations. Border and territorial disputes were common, with the European-imposed borders of many nations being widely contested through armed conflicts.

Cold War conflicts between the United States and the Soviet Union also played a role. When a country became independent for the first time, it was often expected to align with one of the two superpowers. Many countries in Northern Africa received Soviet military aid, while others in Central and Southern Africa were supported by the United States, France or both. The 1970s saw an escalation of violence, as newly independent Angola and Mozambique aligned themselves with the Soviet Union, and West and South Africa sought to contain Soviet influence by funding insurgency movements.

Reparations

Since the mid-1960s there have been calls for reparations to be made to African peoples.

Those calling for reparations argue that financial compensation should be paid to descendants of enslaved Africans by the United States and European governments. They also call for assistance with debt relief, economic development and educational initiatives in those developing countries affected by the slave trade.

Support for reparations is particularly strong in the United States. African American organisations feel that reparations would partially compensate for the stealing of labour and loss of human dignity and human rights to which their African ancestors were subjected.

ABOVE AND BOTTOM RIGHT: The daughters of slaves are educated at a school in Niger. The facility has been set up by Anti-Slavery International and local NGO, Timidria.
© Anti-Slavery International

'If Africa's multiple resources were used in her own development, they could place her among the modernised continents of the world. But her resources have been, and still are being, used for the greater development of overseas interests.'

KWAME NKRUMAH, FIRST PRESIDENT OF GHANA, 1969

Most Black people of African descent have been prevented from achieving progress at the same rate as their white contemporaries. Black people have been discriminated against and disadvantaged in terms of wealth and educational opportunity for the past 300 years.

> I have crossed an ocean
> I have lost my tongue
> From the roots of an old one
> A new one has sprung
>
> GRACE NICHOLS, POET, 1983

Slavery Remembrance Day is celebrated every year in Liverpool and across the African diaspora. UNESCO chose 23 August for the event as it commemorates an uprising of enslaved Africans on the island of Saint Domingue (modern Haiti) in 1791. The image shows Chief Angus Chukuemeka leading a traditional libation on Liverpool's dockside.

Cultural transformations

Every culture is influenced and enriched by others.

Enslaved Africans were forced to deny their own cultures and traditions. They were given new names, foods, clothing, languages and beliefs, but they used the lifestyles and traditions of their homelands to make these new cultures distinctively their own.

African cultures have lived on despite slavery, and they have blended with European and indigenous American traditions to create new and vibrant cultural forms.

Across the Americas and Europe, African cultural influences can be seen everywhere – in religious ceremonies, cuisine, music, language, literature, fashion and festivals. The modern world is imbued with the influence of Africans and those of African descent.

'The sun never sets on the children of Africa'

'Our village once was small but strangers came and spread us all over the world. Now our village is vast and our presence extends to the four corners of the globe. The sun never sets on the children of Africa.'

ALI MAZRUI, ACADEMIC AND POLITICAL WRITER, 1986

There is no continent that does not include Africans, or people of African descent, within its population.

People of African descent outside Africa make up what is known as the African Diaspora. The African Diaspora was created by the dispersal of Africans during and after the transatlantic slave trade. Members of the African Diaspora often share a belief in an African homeland, forged through the collective trauma of slavery, struggle and resistance.

'People need to remember about slavery. It pains the ancestors when we forget.'

MR JOHNSON, GRANDSON OF A SLAVE, SOUTH CAROLINA, 1990

An unquenchable spirit

Despite the trauma of transatlantic slavery, people of African descent have helped shape the society and cultures of the Americas and Europe.

The fusion of African, European and indigenous American traditions has resulted in new and vibrant cultures throughout the world.

The spirit of enslaved Africans, despite efforts by their oppressors to kill it, has survived and lived on through their descendants and their achievements.

RIGHT: Carnival across the African diaspora was created through the fusion of African and European festive traditions.
Photograph: Lee Garland.
© National Museums Liverpool/ Redman Design

African music travelled across the Atlantic with the enslaved people, and modern forms of jazz, hip-hop, rock and rhythm and blues are partly a result of this journey.

Photograph: Lee Garland. © National Museums Liverpool/Redman Design

The International Slavery Museum

The International Slavery Museum opened on 23 August 2007, designated by UNESCO as the International Day for the Remembrance of the Slave Trade and its Abolition, during the bicentenary year of the abolition of the British slave trade. Its predecessor was a groundbreaking display gallery within the Merseyside Maritime Museum, the *Transatlantic Slavery Gallery.* It was opened to the public in 1994 by Dr Maya Angelou, and was seen by millions of people, but ten years later it was suffering from wear and tear.

The bicentenary in 2007 gave us the opportunity to replace the *Transatlantic Slavery Gallery* with a new set of displays that paid more attention to the many legacies of the transatlantic trade, and that also broadened the scope of the gallery to encompass modern forms of slavery and other human rights abuses. This was the origin of the International Slavery Museum. It is the first national museum in the world to deal in detail with the transatlantic slave trade and its legacies.

United Nations Educational, Scientific and Cultural Organization

AN HONOURABLE MENTION OF

THE UNESCO-MADANJEET SINGH PRIZE FOR
THE PROMOTION OF TOLERANCE
AND NON-VIOLENCE

is awarded to

*The International Slavery
Museum in Liverpool*

(*United Kingdom of Great Britain and Northern Ireland*)

in recognition of its efforts to commemorate the lives and deaths of
millions of enslaved Africans, and for its work to fight against legacies of
slavery such as racism, discrimination, inequalities, injustice and exploitation,
as well as against contemporary forms of slavery

Paris, 16 November 2009

Irina Bokova
Director-General

In 2009 the International Slavery Museum received an Honourable Mention as part of the UNESCO-Madanjeet Singh Prize for the Promotion of Tolerance and Non-Violence. This was in recognition of the Museum's efforts to commemorate the lives and deaths of millions of enslaved Africans, and for its work to fight against the legacies of slavery.

23 August is the anniversary of the outbreak of the first successful slave rebellion. On 23 August 1791, an uprising began of the enslaved Africans on the island of Saint Domingue (modern Haiti). This revolt was a crucial event in the fight against slavery. The date is significant as a reminder that enslaved Africans were prime agents of their own liberation.

The Museum's displays seek to increase public understanding of the history of transatlantic slavery, of its many legacies, and of the wider issues of freedom and injustice. The introductory section, the *Freedom Wall*, focuses visitors' thoughts on issues of freedom and enslavement, reminding them of the staggering numbers of Africans taken into slavery through the transatlantic slave trade. From here, visitors progress through a sequence of themes: *Life in West Africa, Enslavement and the Middle Passage* and *Legacy*.

'No one shall be held in slavery or servitude; slavery and the slave trade shall be prohibited in all their forms.'

UNIVERSAL DECLARATION OF HUMAN RIGHTS, 1948

'Freedom is never voluntarily given by the oppressor; it must be demanded by the oppressed.'

MARTIN LUTHER KING, 1963

Untitled #37, Missing Series, 2007/8 is one of a series of photographs by Rachel Wilberforce. The images depict scenes of sex-trafficking and prostitution; a slave trade which still thrives today.
© Rachel Wilberforce

Four centuries of revolts and revolution are examined on the Fight for Freedom and Equality wall, International Slavery Museum.

Photograph: Lee Garland. © National Museums Liverpool/Redman Design

Aims of the International Slavery Museum

- To become the world's leading museum of historical and contemporary slavery.

- To become an active campaigner against human rights abuses and ongoing racism and discrimination in the UK and abroad.

- To develop a world-class academic research programme.

- To offer an innovative educational and learning facility.

- To become a meeting place for the local community to get involved with the issues highlighted by the Museum.

A new resource centre

The next phase of the International Slavery Museum incorporates plans to refurbish and develop the Dock Traffic Office, a building adjacent to the current display galleries. This will become the new International Slavery Museum entrance and will accommodate education and research facilities, a resource centre and community areas. The resource centre will give visitors access to slavery-related digital archives, Black British multimedia and human rights films and documentaries. It will also enable visitors to research family and local history.

'You can only protect your liberties in this world by protecting the other man's freedom. You can only be free if I am free.'

CLARENCE DARROW, US LAWYER, 1920

Enslavement and the Middle Passage, the second gallery in the International Slavery Museum, looks at how enslaved Africans were taken to work on plantations in the Americas. It includes sections on the economics of slavery; life in the Americas and a walk-in audiovisual display about the Middle Passage.
Photograph: Lee Garland. © National Museums Liverpool/Redman Design

Liverpool: capital of the transatlantic slave trade

Further reading

The Interesting Narrative of the Life of Olaudah Equiano, or Gustavus Vassa, the African.

Rediker, M., 2008. *The Slave Ship: A Human History.* Penguin.

Reynolds, E., 1985. *Stand the Storm: A History of the Atlantic Slave Trade.* Allison & Busby.

Sanderson, F. E., 1972. 'Liverpool Delegates and Sir William Dolben's Bill', in *Transactions of the Historic Society of Lancashire and Cheshire*, Vol. 124.

Schwarz, S. and Tibbles, A., 2007. *Liverpool and Transatlantic Slavery.* Liverpool University Press.

Thomas, H., 1999. *The Slave Trade: The History of the Atlantic Slave Trade*, 1440–1870. Simon & Schuster.

Tibbles, A., 2005. *Transatlantic Slavery: Against Human Dignity.* Liverpool University Press.

Walvin, J., 2005. *Black Ivory: A History of British Slavery.* Wiley-Blackwell.

Williams, E., 1944. *Capitalism and Slavery.* The University of North Carolina Press.

Museums and websites to visit

Hadijatou Mani is from Niger. With the help of Anti-Slavery International she successfully sued her government for failing to protect her from slavery.
© Anti-Slavery International

Anti-Slavery International – the world's oldest international human rights organisation
www.antislavery.org

The Gilder Lehrman Center for the Study of Slavery, Resistance, and Abolition
www.yale.edu/glc

International Slavery Museum, Liverpool, UK
www.liverpoolmuseums.org.uk

London, Sugar and Slavery
www.museumindocklands.org.uk

New York Historical Society
www.nydivided.org

National Museum of African American History and Culture
http://nmaahc.si.edu

The Wilberforce Institute for the Study of Slavery and Emancipation (WISE)
www2.hull.ac.uk/fass/wise.aspx

Acknowledgements

Special thanks go to Reverend Jesse L Jackson Sr. for contributing the Foreword to this publication.

Unless otherwise stated all images are the copyright of National Museums Liverpool. The following companies and individuals have kindly provided images for this publication:

The Ancient Brit
Anti-Slavery International
Julius Cruickshank
Etrusia UK
Lee Garland
Liverpool Record Office
Mary Evans Picture Library
Arthur John Picton
Rob Philpott
Prints & Photographs Division, Library of Congress, Washington DC
Redman Design
Simon Webb
Rachel Wilberforce

Text by Dr Richard Benjamin (Head, International Slavery Museum) and Dr David Fleming OBE (Director, National Museums Liverpool)

We would like to thank the following individuals and organisations for their support for the International Slavery Museum. Our thanks also go to those individuals and organisations who wish their support to remain anonymous.

American Friends of National Museums Liverpool, Inc.
Arts Council England (North West)
Barclays Capital
John Bodie OBE & Judith Bodie
Keith Buston
The late Roberta de Joia
Paige deShong Earlam
Xavier Dormeuil
E L Rathbone Charitable Trust
Elderhostel
Barbara Estrin
Gorse Bank Trust
Loyd Grossman OBE FSA
Bert P Headden
JISC
Lady Kaye
Wol & Kerry Kolade
Norman A Kurland & Deborah A David
Sheila MacLeod
National Lottery Commission
Professor Phil Redmond CBE & Alexis Redmond
ShareGift
Andrew Ward

Northwest
REGIONAL DEVELOPMENT AGENCY

dcms
department for
culture, media
and sport

Supported by
The National Lottery®
through the Heritage Lottery Fund

heritage
lottery fund

First published 2010 by
Liverpool University Press
4 Cambridge Street
Liverpool
L69 7ZU

and

National Museums Liverpool
127 Dale Street
Liverpool
L2 2JH

ISBN 978-1-84631-639-5

Design: Axis Graphic Design, Manchester
Print: Gutenberg Press, Malta